BEST OF METALLICA

CLARINET

Recorded by Scott Seelig

Cherry Lane Music Company
Educational Director/Project Supervisor: Susan Poliniak
Director of Publications: Mark Phillips
Publications Coordinator: Rebecca Skidmore

ISBN: 978-1-60378-126-8

CONTENTS

TITLE	PAGE NUMBER	TRACK NUMBER
The Day That Never Comes	3	1
Enter Sandman	4	2
Fade to Black	5	3
Harvester of Sorrow	6	4
Nothing Else Matters	7	5
One	8	6
Sad but True	9	7
Seek & Destroy	10	8
The Thing That Should Not Be	11	9
The Unforgiven	12	10
Until It Sleeps	13	11
Welcome Home (Sanitarium)	14	12
B♭ Tuning Notes		13

The Day That Never Comes

Music by Metallica
Lyrics by James Hetfield

TRACK 1

CLARINET

3

Enter Sandman

Words and Music by
James Hetfield, Lars Ulrich and Kirk Hammett

CLARINET

Fade to Black

Words and Music by
James Hetfield, Lars Ulrich,
Cliff Burton and Kirk Hammett

CLARINET

Harvester of Sorrow

Words and Music by
James Hetfield and Lars Ulrich

TRACK 4

CLARINET

Nothing Else Matters

Words and Music by
James Hetfield and Lars Ulrich

CLARINET

One

Words and Music by
James Hetfield and Lars Ulrich

CLARINET

Moderately

Sad but True

Words and Music by
James Hetfield and Lars Ulrich

CLARINET

Seek & Destroy

Words and Music by
James Hetfield and Lars Ulrich

CLARINET

Moderate Rock
Band

The Thing That Should Not Be

Words and Music by
James Hetfield, Lars Ulrich and Kirk Hammett

CLARINET

Medium Rock

The Unforgiven

TRACK 10

Words and Music by
James Hetfield, Lars Ulrich and Kirk Hammett

CLARINET

Slowly

Until It Sleeps

Words and Music by
James Hetfield and Lars Ulrich

CLARINET

Welcome Home (Sanitarium)

Words and Music by
James Hetfield, Lars Ulrich and Kirk Hammett

CLARINET

More Great Piano/Vocal Books
FROM CHERRY LANE

For a complete listing of Cherry Lane titles available,
including contents listings, please visit our web site at
www.cherrylane.com

See your local music dealer or contact:

EXCLUSIVELY DISTRIBUTED BY

HAL•LEONARD® CORPORATION
7777 W. BLUEMOUND RD. P.O. BOX 13819 MILWAUKEE, WI 53213

Prices, contents and availability subject to change without notice.

1208

METALLICA

Visit Cherry Lane Online at
www.cherrylane.com

Prices, contents and availability subject to change without notice.

MATCHING FOLIOS

...AND JUSTICE FOR ALL
02506965	Play-It-Like-It-Is Guitar	$22.95
02506982	Play-It-Like-It-Is Bass	$19.95
02506856	Easy Guitar	$12.95
02503504	Drums	$18.95

DEATH MAGNETIC
02501267	Play-It-Like-It-Is Guitar	$24.95
02501312	Play-It-Like-It-Is Bass	$22.95
02501316	Easy Guitar	$15.95
02501315	Drums	$19.99

GARAGE INC.
02500070	Play-It-Like-It-Is Guitar	$24.95
02500075	Play-It-Like-It-Is Bass	$24.95
02500076	Easy Guitar	$14.95
02500077	Drums	$18.95

KILL 'EM ALL
02507018	Play-It-Like-It-Is Guitar	$19.95
02507039	Play-It-Like-It-Is Bass	$19.95
02503508	Play-It-Like-It-Is Drums	$18.95

LIVE: BINGE AND PURGE
02501232	Play-It-Like-It-Is Guitar	$19.95

LOAD
02501275	Play-It-Like-It-Is-Guitar	$24.95
02505919	Play-It-Like-It-Is-Bass	$19.95

MASTER OF PUPPETS
02507920	Play-It-Like-It-Is Guitar	$19.95
02506961	Play-It-Like-It-Is Bass	$19.95
02506859	Easy Guitar	$12.95
02503502	Drums	$18.95

METALLICA
02501195	Play-It-Like-It-Is Guitar	$22.95
02505911	Play-It-Like-It-Is Bass	$19.95
02506869	Easy Guitar	$14.95
02503509	Drums	$18.95

RE-LOAD
02501297	Play-It-Like-It-Is Guitar	$24.95
02505926	Play-It-Like-It-Is Bass	$21.95
02506887	Easy Guitar	$15.95
02503517	Drums	$18.95

RIDE THE LIGHTNING
02507019	Play-It-Like-It-Is Guitar	$19.95
02507040	Play-It-Like-It-Is Bass	$17.95
02506861	Easy Guitar	$12.95
02503507	Drums	$17.95

ST. ANGER
02500638	Play-It-Like-It-Is Guitar	$24.95
02500639	Play-It-Like-It-Is Bass	$19.95
02500641	Easy Guitar	$15.95
02500640	Drums	$19.95

S&M HIGHLIGHTS
02500279	Play-It-Like-It-Is Guitar	$24.95
02500288	Play-It-Like-It-Is Bass	$19.95

COLLECTIONS

BEST OF METALLICA
02500424	Transcribed Full Scores	$24.95

BEST OF METALLICA
02502204	P/V/G	$17.95

5 OF THE BEST
02506210	Play-It-Like-It-Is Guitar – Vol. 1	$12.95
02506235	Play-It-Like-It-Is Guitar – Vol. 2	$12.95

LEGENDARY LICKS
AN INSIDE LOOK AT THE STYLES OF METALLICA
Book/CD Packs
02500181	Guitar 1983-1988	$22.95
02500182	Guitar 1988-1996	$22.95
02500180	Bass Legendary Licks	$19.95
02500172	Drum Legendary Licks	$19.95

LEGENDARY LICKS DVDS
A STEP-BY-STEP BREAKDOWN OF
METALLICA'S STYLES AND TECHNIQUES
02500479	Guitar 1983-1988	$24.95
02500480	Guitar 1988-1997	$24.95
02500481	Bass 1983-1988	$24.95
02500484	Bass 1988-1997	$24.95
02500482	Drums 1983-1988	$24.95
02500485	Drums 1988-1997	$24.95

RIFF BY RIFF
02506313	Guitar – Riff by Riff	$19.95

INSTRUCTION

METALLICA – EASY GUITAR WITH LESSONS, VOLUME 1
02506877	Easy Recorded Versions	$14.95

METALLICA – EASY GUITAR WITH LESSONS, VOLUME 2
02500419	Easy Guitar	$14.95

LEARN TO PLAY WITH METALLICA
Book/CD Packs
02500138	Guitar	$15.95
02500189	Bass	$15.95
02500190	Drums	$14.95

UNDER THE MICROSCOPE
02500655	Guitar Instruction	$19.95

PLAYERS

THE ART OF KIRK HAMMETT
02506325	Guitar Transcriptions	$17.95

THE ART OF JAMES HETFIELD
02500016	Guitar Transcriptions	$17.95

METALLICA'S LARS ULRICH
Book/CD Pack
02506306	Drum	$17.95

REFERENCE

METALLICA – THE COMPLETE LYRICS
02501234	Lyrics	$9.99

cherry lane
music company

EXCLUSIVELY DISTRIBUTED BY

HAL•LEONARD®
CORPORATION

7777 W. BLUEMOUND RD. P.O. BOX 13819 MILWAUKEE, WI 53213

0909